America's Leaders

THE **FBI** *Director*

by Scott Ingram

BLACKBIRCH®
PRESS

THOMSON

GALE

San Diego • Detroit • New York • San Francisco • Cleveland • New Haven, Conn. • Waterville, Maine • London • Munich

For more information, contact
The Gale Group, Inc.
27500 Drake Rd.
Farmington Hills, MI 48331-3535
Or you can visit our Internet site at http://www.gale.com

LIBRARY OF CONGRESS CATALOGING-IN-PUBLICATION DATA

Ingram, Scott (William Scott)
The Secretary of Labor / by Scott Ingram.
   pv. cm. — (America's leaders)
 Includes index.
Contents: America's chief enforcement official - The director's many responsibilities — Who works with the director? — Where does the director work? - Who can become FBI director? — A time of crisis — Another time of crisis - A director's day — Fascinating facts - Directors 1908-2003.
  ISBN 1-4103-0090-0
 1. United States. The FBI Director —Juvenile literature. I. Title. II. Series.

Table of Contents

America's Chief Law Enforcement Official

More than 200 years ago, a group of men wrote a document, the U.S. Constitution, which established the American government. The authors of the Constitution divided the government into three separate branches—the legislative branch, the judicial branch, and the executive branch. Under the Constitution, the leader of the executive branch is the president. The president has the power to put laws passed by Congress into effect and to enforce them.

Ever since the first president, George Washington, took office, presidents have had people to advise them. In 1789, the U.S. Congress voted to establish departments in the executive branch to help the president. These were the Departments of State, Treasury, and War. The leader of each department was called a secretary. Together the secretaries formed a group of advisers known as the president's cabinet.

In 1789, Congress also established the position of attorney general. Although this was not a cabinet position, the attorney general was often asked to give legal advice during cabinet meetings. He also advised the president about legal questions and represented the executive branch in cases before the U.S. Supreme Court.

By the mid-1800s, the office of the attorney general had grown as large as that of a cabinet department. As a result, Congress voted in 1870 to create the Department of Justice and named the attorney general the head of the department. This cabinet-level position gave the attorney general control over executive branch legal matters as well as the responsibility for enforcement of federal laws. Crimes that broke federal laws were those that occurred on Native American reservations or during which lawbreakers crossed state lines.

On July 5, 2001, President George W. Bush (left) announced that Robert Mueller (center) was his choice to be the tenth director of the FBI.

By 1870, the attorney general's office had a large staff of lawyers to meet the department's legal responsibilities. The department did not, however, have a force to carry out law enforcement responsibilities. Until the early 1900s, the Justice Department hired private detectives. It also used officers from the Secret Service, which was the Treasury Department force.

In 1907, Attorney General Charles Bonaparte asked President Theodore Roosevelt to create a force of former Secret Service agents and private detectives that would operate under the control of the Justice Department. In 1908, at Roosevelt's request, Congress created the Bureau of Investigation (BOI). The head of the BOI, who reported to the attorney general, was given the title of chief examiner. This act of Congress is considered the beginning of what came to be called the Federal Bureau of Investigation.

Charles Bonaparte

The FBI, created in 1908 to enforce federal laws, today has more than eleven thousand agents who work around the world.

The title of the leader of the BOI was changed from chief examiner to director in 1919. In 1935, the name of the Bureau of Investigation was changed to the Federal Bureau of Investigation.

Today, the FBI is the main law enforcement agency for the U.S. government. It is an organization of more than eleven thousand agents as well as sixteen thousand support workers such as clerks, laboratory technicians, and computer experts. The director of the FBI is considered the top law enforcement official of the U.S. government.

The Director's Many Responsibilities

It is unusual for cabinet members, department supervisors, or agency directors to serve under more than one president. Often, people in such positions leave office when the president they serve under leaves office.

For that reason, the history of the FBI director's position is unusual. From 1924 until 1972, the FBI had just one director, J. Edgar Hoover. Hoover was appointed as the director of the BOI in 1924, and he remained as the head of the FBI until his death in 1972.

During his years of service, Hoover became one of the most powerful men in American government. He created a popular image of FBI agents as honest crime fighters taking on gangsters, spies, and kidnappers. Although the FBI did have success, Hoover also used his position to illegally spy on political leaders and people whose political views he disliked. He also used government money for his own personal expenses.

J. Edgar Hoover became the first FBI director in 1924 and held the job for forty-eight years.

By the 1960s, concern about Hoover's power had become widespread in government. Although the American people were unaware of the director's actions, lawmakers wanted to avoid further abuse of power in the FBI. As a result, Congress passed a law in 1968 that limited the director's term to ten years. The law also required the director to be approved by Congress rather than appointed by the attorney general.

After Hoover's death, news reports revealed that he had kept secret information on political

USA FACT

In 2003, the annual salary of the FBI Director was $141,300.

leaders, including presidents. He had threatened to reveal damaging personal information about anyone who challenged his power or who questioned his use of government funds. Since Hoover's death, one of the main responsibilities of FBI directors has been to restore trust and respect for the FBI.

Today, the FBI director does not have the total control that Hoover once had. In many ways, however, the position carries greater responsibilities. Originally, the FBI was created to investigate crimes such as bank robbery, kidnapping, and car theft, in which criminals crossed state lines. Today, there are more than 350 federal laws that the FBI must enforce.

By the time President John F. Kennedy (seated) was in office, Hoover (rear, center) had become one of the most powerful men in U.S. government.

The FBI is now divided into more than forty different agencies. It has more than 450 offices across the United States. In addition, the FBI has legal attaché offices in fifty-two countries. The agents in the legal attaché offices help train police agencies in foreign countries to prevent crimes that endanger the United States. These crimes include drug trafficking, international terrorism, and computer crimes such as hacking.

As the leader of more than twenty-five thousand employees, the FBI director must make decisions about which crimes require immediate attention. In the weeks after the terrorist attacks of September 11, 2001, for example, the director assigned all FBI agents to determine whether the United States faced additional terrorist threats in the country or abroad. All other crime investigations were given less attention, according to the director's orders.

As it did in the past, the FBI investigates violent crimes that cross state lines. Today, however, the FBI director is also responsible for leading investigations of corporate misconduct, computer crimes, and drug- or gang-related activity. The FBI director also directs investigations of hate crimes and violations of people's civil rights

> **USA Fact**
>
> The FBI keeps more than 250 million sets of fingerprints filed on eight-inch-square cards. If the fingerprint cards were placed in piles, they would equal 133 stacks, each as tall as the Empire State Building.

due to their race or religious beliefs. Finally, since the attacks of September 11, 2001, the FBI also investigates possible terrorist threats in the United States. If terrorists kill Americans in other countries, the director often assigns agents to investigate those crimes.

In modern law enforcement, much of the work of solving crimes or tracking criminals is done in laboratories and on computers. It is the director's responsibility to make certain that the FBI crime laboratories have the most advanced equipment available. It is also critical for the information that is collected to be communicated over a wide area. The director must make certain that information can be distributed to FBI offices as quickly as possible.

FBI director William Sessions (left) used the weekly television program America's Most Wanted *to help capture the agency's most wanted criminals.*

After September 11, 2001, FBI director Robert Mueller had to explain why his agency did not have information that might have prevented the terrorist attacks.

A major part of the director's responsibility each year is preparing a budget for the FBI. This budget is part of the overall budget for the Department of Justice. When Congress reviews the budgets, the FBI director may appear with the attorney general and other Justice Department officials to explain budget requests.

The director may also appear before Congress and other government bodies to explain the actions and the results of FBI investigations. After September 11, the director appeared before Congress to explain why the FBI did not have warnings of such a large terrorist attack.

Where Does the Director Work?

Since 1977, the main office of the FBI director has been located at FBI headquarters in Washington, D.C. The building is also known as the J. Edgar Hoover Building after the longtime director. The building houses eleven different FBI agencies and has office space for more than seven thousand FBI employees. The FBI headquarters has long been one of the most popular tourist sights in Washington, D.C. More than 250,000 people take guided tours through the building each year.

Because the FBI director reports to the attorney general, he regularly spends working hours at the Department of Justice in Washington. The director may also meet occasionally with the president at the White House. He may also be called to appear before the House of Representatives and the Senate.

The director also works at the FBI Academy in Quantico, Virginia, about seventy-five miles south of Washington, D.C. This facility is located on a U.S.

Marine Corps base. The 380-acre academy is the main training complex for all FBI agents. It is also used to train agents of the Drug Enforcement Administration (DEA). Special training of selected police officers from the United States and around the world also takes place there.

The J. Edgar Hoover Building in Washington, D.C., is the FBI headquarters. The FBI director and more than seven thousand employees work in the imposing building.

Sometimes the FBI director meets with the attorney general, who works in the Justice Department headquarters (pictured) in Washington, D.C.

The academy has firearms ranges, defensive driving courses, and physical training facilities. It is also the FBI's center for forensic (criminal) science research. Much of the most advanced scientific work in crime solving is done at this laboratory.

As part of his work responsibility, the director may travel to any of the FBI field offices located in U.S. cities and towns. He may also travel abroad to any of the fifty-two legal attaché offices around the world.

Who Works with the FBI Director?

In most cases, the FBI director reports to the attorney general. In some cases, the director may report to the deputy attorney general. He may also work at the request of other chief officials at the Justice Department.

At the FBI headquarters, the deputy director oversees the everyday operations of the office. In addition to the deputy director, the director works with a chief of staff who sets the director's schedule. Also at FBI headquarters is the general counsel, who is the FBI's chief legal adviser. There are also officers who oversee the department's press releases and other aspects of public information.

FBI director Mueller (right) and Attorney General John Ashcroft (left) worked together to investigate the September 11 terrorist attacks.

At FBI headquarters, the director oversees five main departments and twenty-two offices. The leaders of these areas have titles such as executive assistant directors, assistant directors, and deputy assistant directors.

Who Can Become FBI Director?

Since 1972, only one FBI director has actually served as an FBI agent. In other cases, the nominee has been either a federal judge or a high-ranking lawyer serving the Department of Justice. The attorney general makes the choice of director and recommends that person to the president. The president generally makes a public announcement in which he nominates the candidate for director.

After the candidate is nominated by the president, he appears before the Senate Judiciary Committee. This group of nineteen senators interviews the nominee in a hearing. Next, the committee votes on whether to send the nomination to the full Senate. If the committee approves the nominee, the full Senate then votes. A nominee who receives a majority vote, more than 50 of the total of 100 senators voting in favor, is approved. Once the nominee is approved, he or she is sworn in.

Before Mueller could be sworn in as FBI director, the Senate Judiciary Committee had to approve his nomination and more than half of the full Senate had to vote in his favor.

A Time of Crisis

In the early 1960s, a color line divided black and white Americans in the South. Everything was separated—or segregated—in southern society, from schools to bus stations to drinking fountains.

During these years, African American leaders, such as Dr. Martin Luther King Jr., led marches and peaceful demonstrations against segregation and for civil rights across the South. In no southern city was the struggle for racial equality more violent than in Alabama's largest city, Birmingham. And there was no place that racist whites hated more than the Sixteenth Street Baptist Church. The all-black church was the center for the city's civil rights movement. African American leaders frequently met there to map out plans for demonstrations and marches.

On Sunday morning, September 15, 1963, a powerful bomb was set off in the basement of the church. The blast killed eleven-year-old Denise McNair, along with Addie Mae Collins, Cynthia Wesley, and Carol Robertson, all fourteen years old.

These murders horrified people in the United States and around the world. Because the crime involved explosives and was a violation of federal civil rights laws, more than two hundred FBI agents were assigned

The bomb explosion in the all-black Sixteenth Street Baptist Church in Birmingham, Alabama, killed four young girls and horrified people around the world.

to the investigation. Within two weeks of the bombing, they had strong evidence against four men who had likely planted the bomb.

FBI director J. Edgar Hoover faced a crisis. He had a deep dislike of the civil rights movement. For years, Hoover had spied illegally on civil rights leaders, while doing little to control racist groups such as the Ku Klux Klan.

As a result of his personal prejudice, Hoover ordered the evidence collected by agents in the Birmingham investigation hidden. He removed agents from the case, explaining that the FBI should not become involved in a local crime investigation. He also claimed that civil rights activists had bombed the church themselves to gain public support for their case.

Denise McNair, Carol Robertson, Addie Mae Collins, and Cynthia Wesley (clockwise from upper left) all died in the bomb explosion at the Sixteenth Street Baptist Church in 1963.

Hoover died in 1972. The case remained closed until 1977, when a relative of one bomber turned him in to police. He was tried and sent to prison. In 1996, the evidence sealed by Hoover was released to prosecutors in Birmingham. Two surviving bombers were tried and sent to prison. More than thirty-five years after the murder, justice was finally done.

Hoover's failure to act in a time of crisis, however, severely damaged his reputation. The release of the secret information led many people to request that his name be removed from FBI headquarters.

In 2001, Thomas Blanton Jr. was convicted for the murder of the four girls who died in the Birmingham bombing. He was sentenced to life in prison.

Another Time of Crisis

On December 7, 1941, the Japanese navy launched a surprise attack on American forces in Pearl Harbor, Hawaii. The attack brought the United States into World War II against Japan and Germany. Many Americans, especially those living on the West Coast of the United States, feared that the country would soon be under attack from the Japanese. This fear led to one

Hoover opposed President Franklin Roosevelt's order that all Japanese Americans be evicted from their homes and placed in internment camps during World War II.

of the worst cases of racial prejudice in American history. Soon after the attack, a military commander, John L. DeWitt, accused Japanese Americans of spying and disloyalty. In February 1942, President Franklin Roosevelt ordered all Japanese Americans to be evicted from their homes and placed in internment camps.

Approximately 120,000 Japanese Americans—including more than 75,000 American citizens—on the West Coast were held without charges in the camps. While most officials in the federal government

supported this action, FBI director Hoover strongly opposed it. He saw no evidence that an entire minority group should be held responsible for the actions of a distant enemy.

When Roosevelt asked that Hoover assign FBI agents to track down any Japanese Americans who had avoided internment, the director objected. He did not want the reputation of the FBI to be damaged by association with this government action. Instead, he asked that his agents be used to investigate actual spy cases. Granted that request, the FBI pursued and arrested three German spy rings operating on the East Coast during World War II.

A Director's Day

The FBI director is a busy person whose days are filled with meetings, press conferences, and public appearances both in Washington and in other cities or countries. Here is what a day might be like for the FBI director.

6:00 AM   Wake, shower, read updates of investigation into terrorist killings of Americans in Middle East.

7:00 AM   At work at FBI headquarters; meet with deputy director and chief of staff to preview daily schedule.

FBI director Robert Mueller (right) met with New York City mayor Rudolph Giuliani (left) at Ground Zero after the September 11 attack on the World Trade Center.

8:30 AM   Meet with new Science and Technology Advisory Board for update on installation of wireless technology to allow agents to use handheld computers, laptops, and similar communication devices while still at crime scenes.

10:30 AM   Appear before the Senate Subcommittee on International Operations and Terrorism. Update committee on the FBI's latest procedure for verifying visa applicants' records.

12:00 PM   Travel by helicopter to Philadelphia, Pennsylvania, for an address to the annual convention of the International Association of Chiefs of Police.

3:00 PM   Return to FBI headquarters for press conference announcing the arrest of high-ranking energy executive on charges of illegal stock trading.

5:00 PM   Phone conversation with attorney general concerning the division of responsibilities with the Drug Enforcement Administration (DEA) in the surveillance of a suspected drug manufacturing operation in Florida.

7:00 PM   Dinner with assistant director to review the final version of the report, "Crime in the United States," which FBI compiles and releases each year.

Fascinating Facts

Stanley Finch, director from 1908 to 1912, worked for the Department of Justice in various positions from 1893 until 1940.

William J. Flynn, director from 1919 to 1921, was the only Secret Service agent to serve as director.

William J. Burns operated his own private detective agency before becoming director from 1921 to 1924. After retirement, he had a successful career as an author of mysteries and detective stories.

William J. Flynn

Clarence M. Kelly

Clarence M. Kelly, director from 1973 to 1978, was the only career FBI agent who worked his way up to director. Kelly resigned to become the chief of police in Kansas City, Missouri.

Three FBI directors have served as federal judges: **William H. Webster**, **William S. Sessions**, and **Louis J. Freeh**.

Directors 1908–2003

Stanley Finch 1908–1912

Alexander Bruce Bielaski 1912–1919

William J. Flynn 1919–1921

William J. Burns 1921–1924

J. Edgar Hoover 1924–1972

Clarence M. Kelly 1973–1978

William H. Webster 1978–1987

William S. Sessions 1987–1993

Louis J. Freeh 1993–2001

Robert S. Mueller 2001–

William S. Sessions

Louis J. Freeh

Glossary

adviser—a person who works closely another and provides him or her with information and suggestions

agent—a law enforcement officer of the FBI

attorney general—the cabinet official in charge of the Department of Justice

cabinet—a council of presidential advisers

civil rights—the rights to fair and equal treatment that are guaranteed to all American citizens by federal law

Congress—the legislative branch of the government, composed of the House of Representatives and the Senate

Constitution—the document that established the U.S. government and that contains the principles of the nation

evidence—facts that determine the guilt or innocence of a crime suspect

nominee—a person who has been proposed to fill a certain position

racist—one who supports prejudice and discrimination against those of a different race

Secret Service—a law enforcement group under the supervision of the Treasury Department whose agents also guard the president

Senate Judiciary Committee—a committee of nineteen senators that reviews the executive branch nominees for the Department of Justice as well as federal court positions

For More Information

Books

Balcavage, Dynise. *The Federal Bureau of Investigation.* Minneapolis, MN: Chelsea House, 2000.

Binns, Tristan. *The FBI: Federal Bureau of Investigation.* Oxford, England: Heinemann Library, 2003.

Streissguth, Tom. *J. Edgar Hoover: Powerful FBI Director.* Berkeley Heights, NJ: Enslow, 2002.

Web sites

The FBI Academy
www.fbi.gov/hq/td/academy/academy/htm
Web site with extensive information about the training agents must undergo.

Federal Bureau of Investigation
www.fbi.gov
The home page of the organization with information about directors and famous cases.

FBI Youth
www.fbi.gov/kids/6th12th/6th12.htm
Good page with interactive crime-solving games as well as background information.

History of the Federal Bureau of Investigation
www.fbi.gov/libref/historic/history/artspies/artspies.htm
Web page with good complete story of the founding of the FBI.

Index